50 Forbidden Feasts: Recipes from Vanished Cultures

By: Kelly Johnson

Table of Contents

- Sumerian Honey-Spiced Roast Lamb
- Ancient Mesopotamian Date and Barley Stew
- Minoan Olive and Fig Glazed Pork
- Phoenician Grilled Fish with Pomegranate Sauce
- Carthaginian Honey-Roasted Duck
- Lost Egyptian Spiced Lentil Soup
- Atlantean Herb-Crusted Lobster
- Aztec Cacao-Spiced Venison Stew
- Incan Quinoa and Amaranth Pilaf
- Mayan Smoked Turkey with Chili Cocoa Rub
- Nabatean Fire-Grilled Lamb Skewers
- Olmec Roasted Plantains with Tamarind Glaze
- Khmer Empire Coconut and Lemongrass Fish Curry
- Celtic Honey Mead-Braised Pork Shoulder
- Viking Age Smoked Salmon with Dill Mustard
- Scythian Roasted Horse Meat with Wild Berries
- Göbekli Tepe Ancient Grain Flatbread
- Babylonian Date and Nut-Stuffed Goose
- Hittite Spiced Lamb and Fig Stew
- Ancestral Polynesian Fire-Roasted Breadfruit
- Harappan Lentil and Turmeric Pancakes
- Easter Island Taro and Coconut Soup
- Mississippian Corn and Smoked Bison Casserole
- Aksumite Honey and Berbere Chicken
- Nabatean Rosewater and Pistachio Dessert
- Ancient Japanese Chestnut Rice
- Byzantine Herb-Infused Roast Quail
- Mughal Empire Cardamom-Saffron Rice Pudding
- Lost Amazonian Smoked River Fish with Cassava
- Timbuktu Desert Date and Almond Cake
- Xia Dynasty Fermented Rice and Ginger Broth
- Caral-Supe Civilization Amaranth and Chia Cakes
- Indigenous Taino Cassava Flatbread
- Shang Dynasty Roasted Duck with Five-Spice
- Hellenistic Grilled Goat with Olive Relish

- Tuareg Nomadic Spiced Camel Stew
- Pueblo Ancestral Blue Corn Porridge
- Assyrian Lentil and Pomegranate Soup
- Persian Empire Rosewater and Saffron Custard
- Nabatean Frankincense and Honey-Lacquered Dates
- Muisca Chicha-Marinated Grilled Pork
- Canaanite Herb-Roasted Fish with Lemon
- Lost Khmer Turmeric and Coconut Chicken
- Nuragic Sardinian Chestnut Honey Cake
- Indus Valley Lentil and Wild Mustard Greens
- Cahokia Smoked Duck with Cornbread Dressing
- Tang Dynasty Jasmine-Scented Roast Quail
- Garamantes Sahara Date and Goat Cheese Spread
- Sogdian Spiced Almond and Fig Pastries
- Pictish Wild Boar with Juniper and Heather

Sumerian Honey-Spiced Roast Lamb

Ingredients:

- 1 leg of lamb (4-5 lbs)
- 3 tbsp honey
- 2 tbsp olive oil
- 1 tbsp ground cumin
- 1 tbsp ground coriander
- 1 tsp cinnamon
- 1 tsp black pepper
- 4 garlic cloves, minced
- 1 tsp salt

Instructions:

1. Preheat oven to 375°F (190°C).
2. Mix honey, olive oil, cumin, coriander, cinnamon, black pepper, garlic, and salt into a paste.
3. Rub mixture over the lamb and let marinate for 2 hours.
4. Roast for 1.5-2 hours, basting occasionally, until golden brown.

Ancient Mesopotamian Date and Barley Stew

Ingredients:

- 1 cup barley
- 1 lb lamb or beef, cubed
- ½ cup dates, chopped
- 1 onion, diced
- 2 cloves garlic, minced
- 1 tsp cumin
- ½ tsp cinnamon
- 1 tsp salt
- 4 cups broth

Instructions:

1. Brown meat in a pot with onions and garlic.
2. Add barley, dates, spices, and broth. Simmer for 1 hour.

Minoan Olive and Fig Glazed Pork

Ingredients:

- 2 lbs pork loin
- ½ cup figs, mashed
- ¼ cup black olives, chopped
- 2 tbsp honey
- 1 tsp thyme
- 1 tsp black pepper
- 1 tsp salt

Instructions:

1. Preheat oven to 375°F (190°C).
2. Mix figs, olives, honey, thyme, salt, and pepper into a glaze.
3. Coat pork and roast for 1-1.5 hours.

Phoenician Grilled Fish with Pomegranate Sauce

Ingredients:

- 2 whole fish (such as sea bass)
- ½ cup pomegranate juice
- 2 tbsp olive oil
- 1 tsp ground coriander
- ½ tsp black pepper
- ½ tsp salt

Instructions:

1. Mix pomegranate juice, oil, coriander, salt, and pepper.
2. Marinate fish for 30 minutes.
3. Grill for 4-5 minutes per side.

Carthaginian Honey-Roasted Duck

Ingredients:

- 1 whole duck
- 3 tbsp honey
- 1 tsp cinnamon
- 1 tsp black pepper
- ½ tsp salt
- 1 orange, juiced

Instructions:

1. Preheat oven to 375°F (190°C).
2. Mix honey, cinnamon, pepper, salt, and orange juice.
3. Coat duck and roast for 2 hours.

Lost Egyptian Spiced Lentil Soup

Ingredients:

- 1 cup red lentils
- 1 onion, diced
- 2 cloves garlic, minced
- 1 tsp cumin
- ½ tsp coriander
- ½ tsp cinnamon
- 4 cups vegetable broth

Instructions:

1. Sauté onion and garlic in a pot.
2. Add lentils, spices, and broth. Simmer for 30 minutes.

Atlantean Herb-Crusted Lobster

Ingredients:

- 2 lobster tails
- 2 tbsp butter
- 1 tsp thyme
- 1 tsp oregano
- ½ tsp salt
- ½ tsp black pepper

Instructions:

1. Mix butter with herbs, salt, and pepper.
2. Spread over lobster tails.
3. Broil for 8-10 minutes.

Aztec Cacao-Spiced Venison Stew

Ingredients:

- 1 lb venison, cubed
- 2 cups broth
- ½ oz dark cacao
- 1 tsp chili powder
- 1 tsp cumin
- ½ tsp salt

Instructions:

1. Brown venison in a pot.
2. Add broth, cacao, spices. Simmer for 1 hour.

Incan Quinoa and Amaranth Pilaf

Ingredients:

- 1 cup quinoa
- ½ cup amaranth
- 2 cups vegetable broth
- 1 tbsp olive oil
- ½ tsp salt

Instructions:

1. Cook quinoa and amaranth in broth.
2. Stir in olive oil and salt.

Mayan Smoked Turkey with Chili Cocoa Rub

Ingredients:

- 1 turkey breast
- 1 tsp chili powder
- ½ tsp ground cacao
- ½ tsp cumin
- ½ tsp salt

Instructions:

1. Mix spices and rub over turkey.
2. Smoke for 2-3 hours at 225°F (107°C).

Nabatean Fire-Grilled Lamb Skewers

Ingredients:

- 1 lb lamb, cubed
- 2 tbsp olive oil
- 1 tsp ground cumin
- 1 tsp ground coriander
- ½ tsp cinnamon
- ½ tsp salt
- ½ tsp black pepper
- 2 garlic cloves, minced

Instructions:

1. Mix olive oil, cumin, coriander, cinnamon, salt, pepper, and garlic.
2. Marinate lamb for at least 2 hours.
3. Thread onto skewers and grill for 8-10 minutes, turning occasionally.

Olmec Roasted Plantains with Tamarind Glaze

Ingredients:

- 2 ripe plantains, sliced
- 2 tbsp tamarind paste
- 1 tbsp honey
- 1 tbsp lime juice
- ½ tsp chili powder

Instructions:

1. Preheat oven to 375°F (190°C).
2. Mix tamarind, honey, lime juice, and chili powder.
3. Coat plantains and roast for 20 minutes.

Khmer Empire Coconut and Lemongrass Fish Curry

Ingredients:

- 2 white fish fillets (snapper or tilapia)
- 1 can coconut milk
- 1 lemongrass stalk, chopped
- 1 tsp turmeric
- ½ tsp ginger, grated
- ½ tsp salt

Instructions:

1. Simmer coconut milk with lemongrass, turmeric, ginger, and salt for 10 minutes.
2. Add fish fillets and cook for 8-10 minutes.

Celtic Honey Mead-Braised Pork Shoulder

Ingredients:

- 2 lbs pork shoulder
- 1 cup mead
- 2 tbsp honey
- 1 tsp thyme
- ½ tsp black pepper
- ½ tsp salt

Instructions:

1. Brown pork in a pot.
2. Add mead, honey, thyme, salt, and pepper.
3. Simmer for 2 hours until tender.

Viking Age Smoked Salmon with Dill Mustard

Ingredients:

- 2 salmon fillets
- 2 tbsp Dijon mustard
- 1 tbsp honey
- 1 tbsp fresh dill, chopped
- ½ tsp salt

Instructions:

1. Mix mustard, honey, dill, and salt.
2. Rub over salmon and smoke for 1 hour at 225°F (107°C).

Scythian Roasted Horse Meat with Wild Berries

Ingredients:

- 1 lb horse meat (or beef as substitute)
- ½ cup wild berries (blackberries, raspberries)
- 2 tbsp honey
- 1 tsp black pepper
- ½ tsp salt

Instructions:

1. Preheat oven to 375°F (190°C).
2. Rub meat with honey, pepper, and salt.
3. Roast for 30-40 minutes.
4. Serve with mashed wild berries.

Göbekli Tepe Ancient Grain Flatbread

Ingredients:

- 2 cups einkorn or spelt flour
- ½ cup water
- 1 tbsp olive oil
- ½ tsp salt

Instructions:

1. Mix all ingredients into a dough.
2. Roll into flat rounds and cook on a hot skillet for 2 minutes per side.

Babylonian Date and Nut-Stuffed Goose

Ingredients:

- 1 whole goose
- ½ cup dates, chopped
- ½ cup walnuts, chopped
- 1 tsp cinnamon
- 1 tsp salt

Instructions:

1. Preheat oven to 375°F (190°C).
2. Mix dates, walnuts, cinnamon, and salt.
3. Stuff goose and roast for 2.5-3 hours.

Hittite Spiced Lamb and Fig Stew

Ingredients:

- 1 lb lamb, cubed
- ½ cup dried figs, chopped
- 1 onion, diced
- 1 tsp cumin
- ½ tsp cinnamon
- ½ tsp salt
- 2 cups broth

Instructions:

1. Brown lamb in a pot.
2. Add onions, figs, spices, and broth. Simmer for 1.5 hours.

Ancestral Polynesian Fire-Roasted Breadfruit

Ingredients:

- 1 whole breadfruit
- 2 tbsp coconut oil
- ½ tsp sea salt

Instructions:

1. Roast breadfruit over an open fire until charred.
2. Peel and slice, then brush with coconut oil and salt.

Harappan Lentil and Turmeric Pancakes

Ingredients:

- 1 cup yellow lentils (soaked for 2 hours)
- ½ tsp turmeric
- ½ tsp cumin
- ½ tsp salt
- 1 green chili, chopped (optional)
- ½ cup water
- 1 tbsp oil for cooking

Instructions:

1. Blend lentils, turmeric, cumin, salt, and water into a smooth batter.
2. Heat oil in a pan, pour a ladle of batter, and spread it thin.
3. Cook for 2 minutes per side until golden.

Easter Island Taro and Coconut Soup

Ingredients:

- 2 cups taro root, peeled and cubed
- 1 can coconut milk
- 2 cups vegetable broth
- 1 tsp ginger, grated
- ½ tsp salt

Instructions:

1. Boil taro root in broth until soft.
2. Add coconut milk, ginger, and salt. Simmer for 10 minutes.
3. Blend for a smooth soup.

Mississippian Corn and Smoked Bison Casserole

Ingredients:

- 1 lb smoked bison meat, shredded
- 2 cups corn (fresh or dried, rehydrated)
- 1 onion, diced
- 1 tsp dried sage
- ½ tsp salt
- 2 cups broth

Instructions:

1. Preheat oven to 375°F (190°C).
2. Sauté onion, then add bison, corn, sage, and salt.
3. Pour broth over and bake for 30 minutes.

Aksumite Honey and Berbere Chicken

Ingredients:

- 2 lbs chicken pieces
- 1 tbsp berbere spice
- 2 tbsp honey
- 1 tbsp olive oil
- ½ tsp salt

Instructions:

1. Mix berbere, honey, oil, and salt. Rub onto chicken.
2. Let marinate for 1 hour.
3. Grill or bake at 400°F (200°C) for 25-30 minutes.

Nabatean Rosewater and Pistachio Dessert

Ingredients:

- 1 cup semolina
- ½ cup honey
- ½ tsp rosewater
- ¼ cup pistachios, chopped

Instructions:

1. Toast semolina in a dry pan until golden.
2. Mix with honey and rosewater, then shape into small bites.
3. Sprinkle with pistachios.

Ancient Japanese Chestnut Rice

Ingredients:

- 1 cup short-grain rice
- ½ cup chestnuts, peeled and chopped
- 1 ½ cups water
- ½ tsp salt

Instructions:

1. Rinse rice and soak for 30 minutes.
2. Add water, chestnuts, and salt. Cook covered for 20 minutes.

Byzantine Herb-Infused Roast Quail

Ingredients:

- 2 quails
- 1 tbsp olive oil
- 1 tsp thyme
- ½ tsp oregano
- ½ tsp salt

Instructions:

1. Rub quails with oil, thyme, oregano, and salt.
2. Roast at 375°F (190°C) for 25 minutes.

Mughal Empire Cardamom-Saffron Rice Pudding

Ingredients:

- 1 cup rice
- 3 cups milk
- ½ cup honey
- ½ tsp cardamom
- Pinch of saffron

Instructions:

1. Simmer rice in milk until soft.
2. Add honey, cardamom, and saffron. Stir well.

Lost Amazonian Smoked River Fish with Cassava

Ingredients:

- 2 river fish fillets (tilapia or catfish)
- 1 tsp smoked paprika
- ½ tsp salt
- 2 cups cassava, peeled and boiled

Instructions:

1. Rub fish with smoked paprika and salt.
2. Smoke over wood for 30 minutes.
3. Serve with boiled cassava.

Timbuktu Desert Date and Almond Cake

Ingredients:

- 1 cup dates, mashed
- ½ cup almonds, ground
- 1 cup flour
- ½ tsp cinnamon
- ½ cup honey
- ½ cup water

Instructions:

1. Mix all ingredients into a batter.
2. Bake at 350°F (175°C) for 25-30 minutes.

www.ingramcontent.com/pod-product-compliance
Lightning Source LLC
LaVergne TN
LVHW060134080526
838201LV00118B/3046